Hi!

Many years ago, I got obsessed with finding knowledge for individual and cultural development for our time. As a philosopher (in Norway), ancient Greece was not far away neither in texts, or by plane, walking, feeling and learning, meeting people and getting friends in "ancient Greece." Now I'm very gratefull for taking part in this timeless insight, and share it. I hope you enjoy it too!

I would like to thank everyone who has joined me i Greece, and supported with this project and book; friends, family and radesignstudio.no for making a beautiful book.

Anders

Utterance and development
© Anders P. Petersen 2023
All inquiries about this book are directed to: post@uad.how
www.uad.how
ISBN 978-82-303-5804-7
Graphic design: www.radesignstudio.no

UTTERANCE AND DEVELOPMENT

Dialectics and cultural improvement

Anders P. Petersen

Any improvement of the
human must begin with
knowledge of the human.[1]

1 Bertrand Russell, Sceptical Essays, Routledge 1996 (First edition 1928).

Contents

Introduction

In ancient Greece, the city square was where people met for discussions about politics, philosophy, news, – and any question occupying the citizens' minds.

It's crucial to any cultural improvement that communication is good, and people having similar attitudes towards being members of society.

Our Western culture is the result of a fairly sound cultural basis. However, we still have a distance to go in fully understanding why and how things are improved, and not just by luck and coincidence. There is a fantastic developmental force in people knowing what they're doing, and why they're doing it.

The need for competitive awareness exists not only in companies and organizations, but in all places where individual effort makes a difference.

The involving and developmental thinking had its beginning in ancient Athens, approximately 2500 years ago.

This composition from the fields of history, philosophy, science, pedagogy, and cultural development is relevant everywhere in our society as a basic tool for reason, learning and education.

In order to understand this, you probably expect a certain weight on history, philosophy and deep thoughts. But if their method had been too complex in antiquity, being the major focus in this text, there probably wouldn't have been a cultural cradle. So the simple is often the best.

1.

Innovation

Innovation is based on the foregoing, on experience to discover new things and new thoughts. The ability to do so is not a matter of course.

The best and as far as we know the first on evolutionary thinking in history were the ancient Athenians. They developed an understanding of how to establish a culture of improvement.

Old democratic Athens was by their neighbours seen as ruled by the stupid; the ordinary people who knew nothing. It was at the beginning of the establishment of project democracy, and this for the first time in Europe. The "stupid" were certainly going to surprise everyone.

With ambitions of becoming the best, with a strong common identity, knowledge of the human traits, with pride and courage, contact with other cultures in trade and curiosity, they established our cultural cradle.

The city's freedom and possibilities attracted people and intellectual capacities for discussion, relationships, and collaboration. The culture developed rapidly, increasing involvement, knowledge and skills.

As in antiquity, knowing something commits to a certain degree. Most people won't act against knowing better. So, attitude in thinking is mostly stronger than the negative forces.

It's also ordinary people who in our time is building the future. People who have the opportunity and freedom develop, if there is competence and culture for competition and improvement, and organized for such a goal.

Dialectics and parrhesia
_____

The core discoveries end up with these concepts of anti-quity; *parrhesia* and *dialectics,* where parrhesia represents a cultural framework for attitude, communication and improvement, and dialectics a theory of knowledge growth.

Knowledge of parrhesia was necessary for good dialectics and knowledge-based decisions. These findings are a result of the power of dialectics, breaking concepts, ideas, and objects, into smaller and smaller pieces.

Dialectics originally meant to speak objectively, in both an investigative and exploratory way.

This was a time when the collective knowledge-forming and critical power of dialogue was discovered and institutionalized/organized for an exploratory, critical (scientific), knowledge-promoting, and wise practice.

The key word for our cultural success is simply abstract division; the ability to divide our thoughts, and share them. It's the basis of all knowledge and search for knowledge, critical thinking, participation, improvement, and development of the individual and community.

The main division for good results for people was first and foremost to consider logic/logos, emotions/pathos, good reasons/ethics/ethos, and aesthetics/aestesis; knowledge through the senses, whether something is ugly or beautiful. This was how to become wise, if possible.

In a dialectical conversation (and thinking) there is a dividing of what one is talking about, when asking what someone thinks, whether something can be explained in more detail, or giving notice of shortcomings and errors in what is said.

An investigative practice takes place to find the pieces

of knowledge/parts and connections, relations, and implications of what is the object in conversation.

The tool is language, as we have concepts/ideas for things, and language for meanings and contexts.

Through ideas and words, we reach/see the world, understanding and sharing its constituents and contexts through language.

When you grow up, words are learned every day, and then at school, in subjects, studies, and at work, you are brought into a world of ideas, concepts, focuses, thoughts, and different "realities".

"We grow into language and into the world – these inseparable contexts".[1]

– HANS-GEORG GADAMER

Through logos; language-idea-reality/conditions in the world.

The success factors depend on the mastery of words and their use in engagement, involvement/invitations to speak/ contribute, developing thoughts and ideas, and anchoring a culture, fellowship, and society.

1 From Truth and Method, Sheed and Ward Stagbooks, 1979.

So, the leading power is an important prerequisite for success, but also for stagnation and aggravation.

People in everyday life have different roles, interests, obligations, and a basic morality (ethos) that binds us together. Most people understand the culture, obey the laws, are polite, making an effort where they are. But not everyone is a co-player; and bad moods, apathy, stupidity, greed, cowardice, envy, ignorance, ambition, bad faith, power-hunger, quarrelsomeness, and outright psychopathy, destroys.

Not all cultures are interested in improvement. People and leaders may want things to stay exactly as they are. This has something to do with perspectives, values, beliefs, ideologies, and ignorance. And also; listening to people is for many a risk of losing power and "pride".

Leaders of all sorts; politicians, bureaucrats, HR managers, project managers, friends, fathers and mothers, teachers..., have power. If this power limits expectations of involvement in the "group" or community, the culture will never be aware of what can be achieved.

Man is by nature desires and needs, and must engage to develop, but can also find its place passively. The first step for improving and developing is clear; creating engagement.

Back in Athens' culture, there was a conscious space and expectation of people and talents, redeemed in the struggle against oppression by a greedy and oppressive aristocracy, poor leadership, and war and danger of annihilation, an almost constant state.

They managed to focus on the people's potential, establishing a culture of commitment, having few alternatives, and it was seen as fair to give freedom to the citizens (men). This also created distance to religious faith and tradition, making room for change, the arts, stimulation of the mind, and a more scientific approach to man, politics, and nature.

Aristotle lived at the end of the Golden Age of Athens, observing, collecting, structuring, and specializing the thoughts of his time. His thinking in scientific method is much a fruit of Plato's thoughts on dialectics and knowledge through division.

"(...) For we do not think that we know a thing until we are acquainted with its primary causes or first principles, and have carried our analyses as far as its elements." [2]

— ARISTOTLE

This is highly relevant today, as competition and struggles between individuals, companies, nations and continents, are as they were in antiquity. In short, life is competition for everyone.

---

2 Aristotle Physics 184a10-184a16

From kindergarden to old age and nursing home, it's a competition in being heard, participate, to develop and improve, with ambitions to live as you want, having a good life.

The pursuit of "the good life" is every day, the motivation for individuals, companies, institutions, politics, nations, and geopolitical considerations.

So:

What is most important for cultures that want to develop?

We carefully begin by splitting up how to achieve a development-culture in the least necessary number of points.

1. Knowledge: The most important knowledge is understanding knowledge, and how to lay foundations for knowledge.

2. Attitude: When 1. is in place, it's to ensure that knowledge is used as intended, for a good and common goal. Control of power – good and bad – is important.

3. Objectives: When the objective/goal is clear, one steers towards the objective, using 1. and 2. that constitutes the anchoring in the community/culture/society.

4. Process: Goals and process is the same, as a self-reinforcing mechanism.

Knowledge, attitudes, goals and processes, are based on everyone being free to engage in what they can contribute with. Man achieves meaning, which in turn helps to increase commitment.

The big picture: These four points explain the West as the most technologically developed, where freedom is great, and material prosperity is good. The potential of a culture aware of the importance of the question "how knowledge?" is difficult to predict.

It's the awareness of potential missing that is the portal to knowledge.

The next chapter will show the ideal standard of attitude and expression for improvement, generally speaking.

Chapter 3 will show the essence of method and practice of thinking for thinking, as in point 1 above. Chapter 4 deals with the human consciousness, and its conformity with the method.

2.

The improving utterance

The best conditions for thinking, is without coercion and oppression. The Athenians knew about this and established the concept of parrhesia.

The ideal understanding of a verbal framework is here presented.

Parrhesia

The word parrhesia shows historical awareness, cultural understanding and communication concerning improvement, understanding of power, knowledge of human psychology, development and freedom, and the necessity of a free factual speech. The value of this insight is timeless and unlimited.

Parrhesia means fearless speech. Despite democracy and fine principles such as equal rights and freedom of speech *(isegoria),* it's often difficult to speak in real life, because of the risk of reprisals. People can hinder experiential statements, knowledge, and legitimate questions.

To avoid negative power, punishment, and retaliation, many therefore choose to be "loyal", consenting and silent. To only express the obvious and let oneself be ruled by fear and strategy, power will increase to, and in, fewer hands, and the desire to express oneself will decrease, and we will end up being ruled by the few. The few does not represent development, but stagnation.

The will to improve lies in the attitudes of the involved, participants and inhabitants, and success presupposes a platform of common values.

The democratic society in Antiquity wanted to promote formation *(paideia)* according to the rules of parrhesia; utterance and participation, to strengthen wisdom, and community.

If speaking while being the inferior power in a relationship, parrhesia gives "cultural protection". In this context, potentially, possessors of power are all who can make it difficult for the individual to speak about what is right and sensible. It can be friends, class and schoolmates, family, colleagues, bosses and leaders, bureaucrats, and so-called "correct thinking." When talking at risk you always say something important, or you are stupid.

Traditional methods for how unwanted factual speech are encountered are different ruling techniques: Ignoring and silencing, building alliances, bullying and threatening, backbiting, dishonest allegations, changing the topic of conversation, ridicule, pointing out disloyalty, threaten with personnel matters or investigations, threat of being fired. All this creates fear for your future, and career.

It represents the tyranny, because it's unreasonable, as you are exposed to something you can rarely defend yourself against.

This is the power of the ignorant, the individualist, who in this context becomes the tyrant.

"It is a slave's life not to have the right to speak (...) Then one must endure the idiocy of those who decide (...) One finds that it pays to deny one's nature, and become a slave."

– EURIPIDES

In Athens' heyday, risky statements were to come from honorable and courageous men, as role models.

He who spoke knowledge at risk was a parrhesiastes, in danger by virtue of his utterance, and thus in an inferior power. But leaders, even with great power, can also speak at risk. Telling the truth to the people can be risky, like a political leader presenting unpopular advises and politics. When this happens, the people are the tyrants.

But speaking at risk to the people is also the hallmark of good leaders. Good leaders are good leaders because they are brave, listen, and are willing to take responsibility/lead, telling the people the truth in good faith, despite the risk of people's power as a group.

Ordinary people also backbite and engage in hidden tyranny, bullying against each other. It was not always the case that the people represented "the good" and "the truth." A people without knowledge can be a disaster for a fellowship.

In the parrhesia perspective, the duty of wisdom is stronger than the right to speak. You don't have an ethical right to speak if it's to bully, or what you say is wrong, or a lie.

Parrhesia was not only a right, but also a duty based on conscience. The democratic citizen had a duty to speak out for the benefit of the community.

With no brave men and women (today), tyranny will prevail in families, schools, society, organizations, politics, religion, bureaucracy, public opinion, countries,.... wherever there are people.

It was the square in Athens (agora) that became the important center for expression and debate, reflection, and engagement. Here lay also the political and juridical institutions. Philosophers like Socrates had daily discussions with philosophers, rhetoricians/sophists, and others. The square had an open thematic, engaging and socially role, anchoring the culture.

After the first phase of democracy, they introduced a limit for free speech in Athens. It was forbidden to say things that could harm democracy, such as lies, inaccuracies and statements of great individual interest, called graphè paranomon (write/say illegal).

They feared that confidence in expression and the free speech could be abused. They made it criminal to propose "harmfull laws", and/or misleading the people. The punishment could be everything from fine to death (as with Socrates).

But of course, this increased risk for the speaker was also abused by claiming to "speak the truth in danger". It's a great tool for attacking true speakers, and "winning" a debate. We can recognize this in our time.

Here is an answer from the moderate democratic politician Diodotus to Cleon (political traditionalist), who thought that talking and discussing was not as good as practical action.

Diodotus was aware of people who showed "passion with vulgarity and irrationality."

"As for the argument that speech should not be the exponent of action, the man who uses it must be either senseless or dishonest/ insecure: senseless if he thinks he can use another medium; dishonest/insecure if he wants to carry a shameful goal and doubts his ability to speak well in a bad case, and thinks he can scare opponents and listeners with well intentioned slander."

(...) "I think that two things that are most opposed to good advice and debate are haste and passions; haste goes hand in hand with folly, passion with vulgarity and irrationality. (...) The good citizen should excel not by intimidating his opponents, but by beating them fairly with argument." [1]

– DIODOTUS

The parrhesia-norm allowed people to express themselves about things where they were. Thinking about wholeness, social order, human nature and cleverness, made the methodological way to knowledge, a common concern and practice.

Parrhesia thus stands as evidence of this insight, as it shouldn't be a democracy just by name. It wasn't to be the case that the culture consisted of old power structures, mythology and ideas, where only the "best", the aristoi/ aristocracy, was to express itself, being in power.

But, thoughts about the neighbor's private life, one should keep quiet about. The other's freedom does not concern one's own freedom/leisure.

"We do not resent the neighbor if he lives according to his own desires, and we do not make life difficult for him with

---

1   Thucydides, Diodotus; Speech for Mytilene.

crooked glances, which may
not hurt anyone, but which
are still annoying." [2]

– PERICLES

Using these principles today, with real freedom of speech,
with respect and objectivity, we get a dialectic between
conversational people that constitutes the harmony of
opposites, and this can create an incremental process of
improvement in the individual and everywhere, from top
to bottom in society.

"Ok, so speak!"

We live in a culture that makes it difficult for people to have
deciding power, besides organized free political elections.
But the insight and awareness of the shortcomings exists,
or will appear in the consciousness of individuals, and *there*
is the way to development and the good solutions.

"...and instead of looking at
discussion as a stumbling block in
the way of action, we think it an

---

2 Pericles Funeral Oration, Thucydides.

indispensable preliminary to any
wise action at all." [3]

– PERICLES

Below are the rules for parrhesia:

RULES (normative)

Parrhesia requires courage, honesty, knowledge and insight.

Everyone must:

- have the right to speak

- speak nicely

- tell the truth, what is right

- argue objectively and seek insight

- talk about what is important, even if it may be disadvantageous for himself

- listen to those who have something to contribute to the case

- not flatter

3   Pericles Funeral Oration, Thucydides.

- not backbite

- not talk only for self-interest

- not endanger the person giving the right to speak

In addition, the leaders of the people shall:

- serve the people

- listen to and learn from the people to strive for wise choices

- respect that the authority over the people must rest on the attitude of the wise

- take responsibility for the people

- speak and express themselves to the people

3.

To the point, what?

Gaining knowledge.

Plato was Aristotles teacher. His quote below shows our culture's first, highest and generalized insight into what the path of knowledge is based on, as opposed to belief.

" ...but the clear waking vision of it is impossible for them as long as they leave the assumptions which they employ undisturbed and cannot give any account of them. For where the starting point is something that the reasoner does not know, and the conclusion and all that intervenes is a tissue of things not really known, what possibility is there that assent in such cases can ever be converted into true knowledge or science? (...) is not dialectics the only process of inquiry that advances in this manner, doing away with hypotheses, up to the first principle itself in order to find confirmation there?" [1]

---

1 Plato, The Republic 533c.

"(...) Do you agree, then, said I, that we have set dialectics above all other studies to be as it were the coping-stone – and that no other higher kind of study could rightly be placed above it."[2]

This is the core of the development for thought and society, and:

"(...) Then you will provide by law that they shall give special heed to the discipline that will enable them to ask and answer questions in the most scientific manner."[3]

– PLATO

The existential seriousness of not having knowledge is quite clear to Plato. It's vital. You must be invited, engaging socially, asking questions to gain knowledge, to develop and contribute. To develop, it's important to engage

---

2 Plato, The Republic 543e.

3 Plato, The Republic 534d.

in questions and put forward own thoughts. Without knowledge, you simply don't know what you don't know, and you are closed for thinking. Language is the portal to thinking.

Plato said that thinking is like talking to oneself. If you talk with others, it assists your own thinking.

To think is to be open to the shortcomings of one's inner dialogue, and our consciousness is by nature intuitive in an investigative way. Its very essence is to ask for meaning.

The formal knowledge in this chapter constitutes the methodological grounding, realized by good attitudes.

Plato's dialectic forms a starting point for objective thinking about thinking, saying it's not enough to agree on what's right, or to believe that one has knowledge.

This "pinnacle of all sciences" is to know how to acquire knowledge. If you have this knowledge, there is more confidence in thinking and knowing behind what, how, why, which, who, and when.

It's essential in all sciences to focus/to speak factually; to speak dialectically. To speak factually/objectively is implicitly – although often unconsciously – to investigate something. When you talk about something, you (actually) make claims about how things are.

It involves/takes place a division of the object of conversation, and perhaps down to the smallest components, as will be shown in the following.

That is why attitudes to anchoring objectivity, truth and honesty are so important.

Development is thus dependent on four things: absence of strong beliefs, practice/knowledge of the foundation of development, good attitude, and what people communicate.

The dialectical prosess can have this structure (below) to visualize, a model which is easy to remember.

Dialectics:

$$\text{T} \_\backslash \_ \overset{\text{S}}{} \text{AT}$$

This is explained as follows:

1. T: Thesis is believing something or claiming something. This is how we usually talk about things, explaining something. An utterance is a thesis, holding something true.[4] (It doesn't have to be important, or science).

2. AT: Anti-Thesis is the opposite, or discovery of deficiency/ contradictions/ignorance. It means in everyday life that we disagree with someone, or that something is missing in what the other person says. We simply find a mistake or add something that is missing.

3. S: Synthesis is a "union" of the T and the AT. Out of these combinations, our consciousness lacks knowledge which is "filled", even often before we know it. New

---

4 When we utter something, it's the natural and necessary purpose of language, that what is said by someone is true, or/and that they believe it true, though often not.

ideas emerge, a combination/synthesis of old ideas and its ATs; "opposites". We discover something new, or someone says something we didn't know or have thought of before. In the synthesis, we have become a little smarter. It goes to a higher level (S).

The dialectical arrangement is a kind of *harmony of opposites,* the words of the philosopher Heraclitus.

Antithesis means in Greek "that which is the opposite", originally a rhetorical device to clarify a point, from pre-democratic (archaic) times. When you say what something is not, it also becomes clearer what is, what you mean.

This method and structure of claims and contradictions for learning applies to all conditions in the world. The art of questioning is the art of how to understand something, how things work or do not work, what something is made of, how something develops, collapses, cracks, melts, disappears, and how to understand this, whatever it is.

All these are changes from what they were first, to what they are. In fact, the way our consciousness sees things and the world, is to look for lacks/defects/or potential improvement, or to confirm what is. Therefore we (fortunately) often discover new things when we do not expect it.

```
_____
 _____\
  _____\
   _____
    _\__\_
    T_\_ AT
```

This (above) is how knowledge grows dialectically "from below". Here, the first idea is spread, which in turn forms more.

"Knowledge always means, precisely, looking for contradictions. (...) Knowledge is dialectical from the bottom up. Only a person who has questions can have knowledge, but questions include the antithesis of "yes", or "no", as being in one way or another." [5]

– HANS-GEORG GADAMER

To ask is to think, and to think is to have an inquisitive attitude. To think is to be active. In our inner world we can miss something, wish for something, discover, remember, look forward to something, and fear something. All this is not, which is not here in time, but which we think about and relate to curiously.

The following presents the core of ancient development, knowledge, scientific thinking, and methods:

---

5 Hans-Georg Gadamer, Truth and Method 1979.

We are engaged in ourselves through the awareness of our inner world, with our body living and acting with the surroundings of our outer world. When we think about what something is, the something is concepts/ideas/typifications of things.

The words are tools we think with, having them in our heads/minds. Our understanding of things and even the entire world is conceptual. (Is thinking possible without words?) It's difficult to think of it in any other way. They constitute a logical connection, so that the world outside us is understandable to us.

These words represent classes/categories of things which we mostly agree on, taught when we learn our languages, meaning what they mean. It allows us to talk meaningfully together.

If you do not learn words and their use, then you are excluded from a community, a community of basic understanding.

A developing fellowship is based on an agreement on division and arrangement of things and ideas:

Definitions/classifications

Concepts/classifications are clarifying tools of thought; what we think about and talk about, always. Words are classifications *(taxonomy)* of things in the world we basically agree on, or not. Learning is new discoveries of words/ideas and contexts in these classes/bags of concepts, or we invent, create, or establish new words.

A thing we call something (word/name) is in Greek taxon,

which contains a meaning, a definition, e.g., car, battery, horse, etc. Learning is a discovery, hearing or experiencing a new phenomenon, or a new insight, where one forms the basis of ideas for understanding.

Today, it's strange to think that classifications of things as a conscious cultural knowledge/scientific improvement, was created at some point. Aristotle has been given the credit for this work, but initiated by Socrates and Plato.

It's the definitions and categories that give us habitual thinking, but this unfortunately also has the potential for inhibiting new knowledge, when we believe in and rely on our pre-understanding and end up being locked on certain definitions and categories.

Division/diairesis

Since our world consists of concepts/objects, and our culture is interested in understanding this world, we divide it into parts, to see and understanding its relations.

A thing, a whole thing, which we see as an "own thing" *(holon)*, is such as a car, mobile, economic, dinner recipe, etc. Things has its own names (taxon).

It's dividing *(diairesis)* that allows us to see what things are made of. A car is an engine/battery, body, wheels, seats, screws, fasteners, cables, and so on. Mobiles are battery, plastic, glass, data chips, et cetera. Nature is bees, flowers, animals, clean water, sun, wind, rain, gases, atoms ....

In economics, it's looking at products, costs, what's possible to make money on, why it's quality, et cetera. To have a Michelin Star, the chef must know everything about the food, taste, and service.

When we have a future goal, we fantasize about the future and see which "parts" must be included.

We go "into" the ideas (about the things/objects) and thus also the concepts, "seeing" what we do not know or understand (logos). This exercise is part of/included in the dialectic, a factual "critical" and investigative process. We see how the concepts and words "follows" things (holon) in the world as labels (taxon), where they "hang" in our consciousness as something (objects) we can think of and use with others towards a common goal, to understand.

Behind the practice of diairesis is the ancient Greek understanding of a world of things consisting of parts, all the way down to what only the mind/ideas can logically relate to, as in the philosophical scientific atomism from ancient time.

Atom means in Greek the smallest undividible parts, a conceptual "proof" and a good example of how early thinking in physics/nature is representative of the development of scientific thinking.

The world/reality is made up of these parts/atoms, and the wholes and contexts they are part of. In the subject of physics, it's precisely dividing that forms the basis for certain knowledge. In atomism, the power of thought is made logical, which ends with the term atom, Gr. the undividible/the smallest.

It's a drive, a strong desire to know the world and how to understand it. This is what particularly sat the Greeks apart from other cultures.

So here we see an example of the early scientific thinking,

which is not just scientific thinking, but also an ideological daily attitude towards a factual behavior which synthesizes the social and communicational with the scientifical, our cultural goal.

Below we go into detail on what the first principle means, such as dividing objects.

Model of things/ideas in reality:

The big X is a thing/concept belonging to a class, and the plural smaller x's are parts of the thing.

If the top X is the main object/concept of what we are going to investigate, such as a battery, rocket, idea of improvement, car, human, shoe, business model, science, or whatever, – the parts of an object are as follows:

Contexts/Meronomy

Going deeper in understanding: These parts are connected and work together. The ancient concept of striving to understand parts-relationships for the whole was meronomy, *meron*; part – onuma; name.

Meron means part-relation. The world consists of things of

parts, contexts, and processes, for which we already have words/concept, or must create to be able to understand.

A deeper understanding of the parts involves how they connect and intervene and work on each other to create wholes/functional things.

Model of relations between parts in a thing.

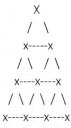

The meron-perspective is to understand how these parts "hang"/work together, illustrated by the lines between the x's.

Below a figure of notions/knowledge of four things that connect as a whole, with their (sub) parts.

The question comes first: What is it, what is the purpose, how does it work, how can we explain, what should we do, how can we cope, who and what do we need?

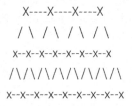

The deeper the understanding behind the concept, object, project or plan, the more knowledge and power there is to succeed.

The words/ideas, the thoughts and what we say about them, give "access" to the thoughts as a reflective process about things and conditions. Through language we share them, and reality.

Logos

One concept that covers these mindful exercises is logos; words and expressions that says something about the world. When someone says something, our consciousness (which has learned what words and expressions mean) will first unconsciously ask if what is said is correct. If we know what's talked about, we can immediately say whether something is true or not, or whether it seems reasonable.

One of the important discoveries in the development of logos, was that a word is not the thing, in a way, but that the word is something other than the thing, or what one is talking about. This opened to see that things could be different than how you understood them.

A word is an artificial conceptual idea(lization), using signs/ letters, making a word, and explanations to fill (definition) the word with its meaning. A thing's designation is therefore random. It could be called something else, and so the meaning of the word can be understood differently, and so "the truth" about it.

A modern scientist (or anyone) will experience the same thing discovering something new and must give words to this/these, based on the understanding and the ideas provided. Here the scientist suddenly "reaches behind," transcending what was previously seen as a (learned) matter of course.

It's the same discovery that words are arbitrary, in the sense that all words can be recreated, like people's names. You "are" not your name, distinguishing between things and words, things and labels. This discovery was the first step in becoming analytical, having distance to the thing; what is something "really"?

Logos/logic is a word/concept that covers our consciousness of wanting to find (understand) connections between words, sentences and expressions, our idea/notion of what is talked about, or whether our ideas is correct and corresponds to (our ideas of) reality.

It's not logical to speak as if you know if you don't. So simple, so logical, but also so easy to forget in a world of speed and efficiency, and the need for knowledge and certainty.

A model of knowledge growth, and cultural factors:

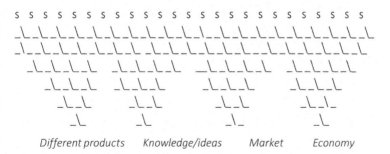

Different products   Knowledge/ideas   Market   Economy

Mobiles / prod: Knowledge, battery/metals, com.technology.
Opportunities: Politics, knowledge, networks and resources, profit.

Above, the logical element is that knowledge is based on knowledge about a world of things, simple and straightforward. It's a growth, a dialectical growth, as the quote by Gadamer refers to.

As we see, the level of knowledge increases rapidly. It's a compilation of the dialectical figure. For this to be possible, knowledge and ideas, politics, economy, and attitudes must be in place, constituent as culture.

If we look again at the model for meronomy and put several together, we see its similarity to the model turned upside down, if we imagine that we examine several objects/things/anything. Then we gain knowledge in breadth and depth, and we can say that we understand. With knowledge, the ideas in our head's mirrors reality.

Reality is divided into categories, "subclasses", parts and contexts, corresponding to an increasing amount of knowledge and specialization.

So schematically (below) we have the birth of the idea of a "coherent world", where ideas and knowledge rests on the others as a construction.

The figure below is to illustrate ideas, as man experiences and systematizes it.

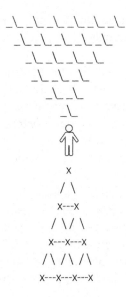

```
_____\
 _____\
  _\_\_\_\_\
   _\_\_\_
    _\_\
     _\
      ♀
      ⇑
      
      X
     / \
    X---X
   / \/ \
  X---X---X
 /\ /\ /\
X---X---X---X
```

What we have in our heads, is the "sum" of our orientation towards the world/reality, and our engagement and ideas about it.

Everything that is "under the feet" is our concepts of the "outside" of our heads/reality; our reality as it appears, as we know it by dividing it up, finding designations for the notions and ideas, and the knowledge we gain about this/things. What is above the head and under the feet is "reflected"/"mirrored".

When we speak objectively, we present and discover the parts, connections, and cause-effects of things, if we are thorough, critical and analytical.

It's all our notions of our real (subjective) reality, which we in language and action connect to an intersubjectivity, a fellow understanding.

Now we have looked at the "secret" recipe and attitude of this culture, and not only among the Athenians.

The Athenians, interested in their surroundings, and with ambitions of becoming the best city to live in, managed to systematize it, making the political system, economy, and culture aware of this. It was not only thinkers/philosophers and scientists who, with the help of this abstract and conceptual dividing method, understood nature.

It concerned a general approach to the universe, mathematics, acoustics, the human and existence, philosophical method, reason and logos, communication, participation and expressing conditions, art, theatre and drama, architecture, aesthetics, urban planning, martial arts, weaponry, warstrategy, diet, health, medicine, and more.

As an example of a scientific and empirical demonstration of how effective communication is for knowledge sharing, I would like to refer to a modern example.[6] The scheme below is a large "step on, meet and spread knowledge"-sheet to lay on the floor to demonstrate how knowledge is spread effectively.

The sheet is part of an algorithm research demonstration of how computer algorithms work, and how humans (actually) spread knowledge in the same way.

The example is based on that only one person has the right knowledge. Everybody's walking in the same direction. The knowledge-person shares at the meeting points/circles what he knows. The person the knowledge-person has met conveys at the next point, three (1,6)

---

6 Prof. Michael Ralph Fellows. Department of Informatics, University of Bergen, Norway.

and four times, until they're all come to the other side having the right knowledge.

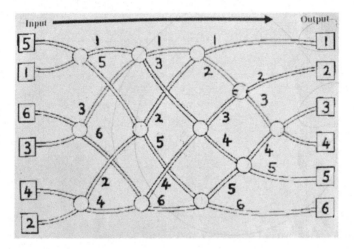

The demonstration provides an empirical understanding of the power of dialectics, and a communication culture. It gives a magnificent picture of the power of people meeting in ethos, pathos, and logos; a goal, and communication/engagement.

Below we see how different competencies form wholes of new things/new competencies. This illustrates knowledgebuilding.

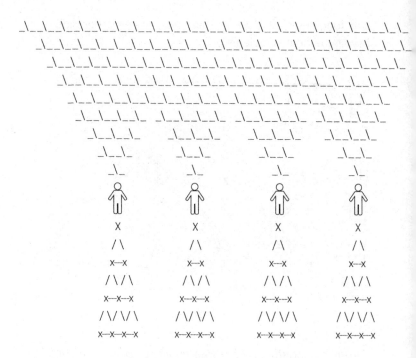

If we show that new ideas often imply people, we get this form:

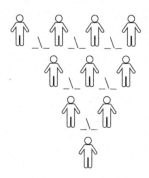

The growth is even more potential than this illustrates, as each person in each meeting shares it with one, as such; 1, 2, 4, 8, 16, 32, 64, 128, 256, 512, etc. Here we see that knowledge-growth is intersubjective to have people's potential. It's in the others that you find the knowledge you don't have yourself.

As said earlier, talking with people implies a certain basic logic. We expect people to speak reasonably true, and that they know something about what they say.

Attitude to knowledge: As critical people, we will have reasonable doubt if we ourselves do not have any insight into what is presented. This is even more challenging listening to specialists or people we believe have good insight. We are in "danger" when we need to believe in something. Any theory can become a belief system that closes our minds.

But how do we establish knowledge in our heads? Through experience, theory, and logic?

In most cases it's all three parts. We experience and "check" with what we knew before, or what we thought we knew before. We don't always know that we know something. Much of our knowledge don't exist as a conscious scientific certainty.

Our intuitive natural basic logic, mapped and classified/ conceptualized, are these:

Verification

Verification is to show that something can be right, and so provide greater security for something. It can be to indicate that the oven is hot, by feeling that the oven is hot. A widely used example in scientific theory is that, at some point the belief was that all swans are white, as all observed swans were white. That was up until black swans were discovered, rendering verification somewhat moot as a knowledge test.

A current example could be that wind turbines are good for the environment and energy production. The division of what and how as a potential falsification, gives the answer to why building windmills didn't go as planned, and partly why energy is very expensive.

Falsification

Falsification shows that something is wrong. Proving something wrong provides greater knowledge, as knowing something wrong is better than believing something right. To point out that the oven is hot, to feel that the oven is cold is a falsification.

In the swan-example, the claim or belief is falsified by the fact that there are black swans in Australia.

The wind turbine example points out that it has unforeseen negative effects, contributing to a European energy crisis because of "too little wind," that other energy production no longer exists (nuclear power plants), that electricity becomes too expensive for people, and destroying surrounding nature, the beautifulness (aesthesis), and wildlife. Confidence in politics and a promising sustainable future is falling. The "fact" that wind turbines are only positive is falsified.

One way we often use both verification and falsification

at the same time, is when predicting what is going to happen based on an assumption as in "this is heavier than water and will sink". If the item sinks the claim is verified, and if it floats, it's falsified.

Premises and conclusion

A conclusion is always logically the sum of its premises, otherwise it's just a belief in something. This goes straight back to Plato's quote on dialectics.

P1, P2, P3, P4, ... = K.

If you go from K and back to its premises, it's a deduction. This is quite reminiscent of the dividing, of a matter into its existing parts.

Syllogism

The syllogism scheme is different, as the conclusion follows from another logical form.

P1	Socrates is human
P2	All human beings are mortal
Conclusion:	Socrates is mortal

The form:

A (Socrates) B (human)	A - B
B (human) C (mortal)	B - C
Conclusion: A (Socrates) C (mortal)	A - C

Because the logical scheme is a form, you can enter anything and get a "correct" but wrong conclusion. This logical form can quickly deceive us believing something wrong if the premises are not true:

Example:

P1   All people are bananas
P2   Bananas hang in trees
Conclusion: All people hang in trees

The form is the same:

A - B
B - C
A - C

These logic forms are an offspring of a dialectical thinking.

If we want to find knowledge, insight and truth, the attention must be on the level of detail, the premises "the little things", their context, and let us not be fooled by logical tools. Logic can be treacherous when it comes to finding the first principles and truth.

Definitions: We often use words without being aware that we mean different things, both of single words and expressions. So, first in any discussion, it must be clear what we are talking about, that it's the same (same class/concept/taxonomy).

A state of knowing-not-knowing; humbleness.

To "loosen up" we must look beyond/exceed that we think we know "anything". Therefore, the belief-for-safety-thoughts must be set aside; put in parentheses (epochè in philosophical phenomenology), and ask; what do I really know?

When we grow up in the world, we believe and assume a lot, moving us into the unknown and develop. Growing into the world, we try to explain and understand, making assumptions for ourselves into what we unreflectively believe *(doxa)*. Although not in a broad perspective avoidable, our goal is to be aware of belief as belief.

By reading this book for example, we want to find ways of thinking that can stimulate for new ideas. Maybe you "knew" what thinking and development is but could not articulate it. Well, now you can. Now you already have more knowledge (episteme) about this.

Power and participation

Getting rid of negative power was an important motivation in Athens to develop a new culture. In human history, the forces for and against doing things better have always been the same.

Thinking well together presupposes that there is equality and recognition between those who communicate. Thinking well within unfree frameworks requires courage, a quality that is not fairly distributed between people.

By participating verbally in a fellowship, one must take a stand in the social context which one is part of. You think differently together with someone, with greater awareness of the quality of thinking. The reason is that you must structure what you have to say, thus mistakes and shortcomings is more easily revealed to oneself and others.

"I have made my statement; if it is wrong, your business is to examine and refute it. But if, like you and me on this occasion, we were friends and chose to have a discussion together, I should have to reply in some milder tone more suited to dialectic. (...) Tell me, is there something you call an end? Such a thing, I mean, as a limit, or extremity – " [7]

– SOCRATES

In cultures without freedom of thought, due to tradition, religion, theories, faith and belief, tyrannical leaders, and otherwise dominant personalities, little happens.

Things will be as they are, until they eventually crash, are destroyed or outcompeted. Below is "the line" (no innovation) in cultures of faith and tyrannic power. It's the same (timeless) forces whether it's an individual, a company, nation, or region.

T: --→

7 Plato, Menon 75d.

It's easy to be fooled. Some cultures are seemingly innovative, with richness to buy from the dialectical culture, or copy (spying) products and thinking, but have developed little themselves.

History shows that the developmental potential of traditional/religious cultures is limited.

However, development takes place as one is open to influence, which contributes to creative power/ constructive contradictions, and competitiveness. This is freedom as curiosity, humbleness, courage, and ambitions.

Without ability to adjust, keeping your eyes open, to be interested and learn, you don't take part in the competition for development and survival.

Knowledge-cultures

Innovative cultures does not come by itself.

To achieve effective knowledge, growth and improvement, one must have a method/awareness and attitude for it.

Based on the division, classifications, knowing relations and interacting parts in the world, a knowledgesharing culture was established, that motivated and drove an analytical process. Conscious understanding of shortcomings and needs, comes from concepts that forms a focus.

An awareness for e.g., "lack of knowledge" can't have a common focus unless we have a concept of lack of knowledge.

The Athenians of antiquity had several knowledge promoting and culture forming concepts as; episteme, techne, sophrosyne, parousia, and the harmony of opposites.

To begin with the latter first:

Deficiency/Parousia

Parousia means presence, as the presence of a deficiency, like an emptiness. That is just genius, because: In our consciousness, it's like a hole in our knowledge as a nothingness, a not-knowing, a lack in the "object" of knowledge. Only fools will try to cover up what one doesn't know, trying to remain ignorant.

The harmony of contradictions.

This parousia-meaning above has its origin in the view that improvement and development have their power in opposites.

An important contradiction is precisely the discovery of non-knowledge as opposed to knowledge, and otherwise all elements of contradictions and extremities in nature, which when they meet gives pleasure as a golden mean. It implies a harmony of opposites.

Below is the figure with a "nothingness", to show the seriousness of lack/the presence of a hole, as a nothingness.

The hole must be discovered before it can be closed, at the expense of time, money, and other values.

In the next figure, the "missing person" may, e.g., be this

ancient knowledge of improvement-thinking which for 2400 years has been forgotten, but here about to return, approx. 400 years after the Enlightenment.

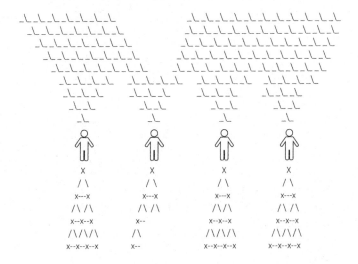

The missing person visualises a lack of an essential part of an ideal whole/unpresented knowledge, e.g., ignorance, because of speaking at potential risk, or the feeling of having to speak at risk, and lack of conceptual awareness in the unfree society.

So, communication and development can't be seen independently of the power-relations that are played out between the involved. If someone becomes too dominant, others will not make their input.

In dialogue and debate, finding shortcomings and potential for improvements, the goal is not to win, but to improve. In potentiality for war, if you don't have the skills and equipment to defend yourself, you will be defeated/crushed.

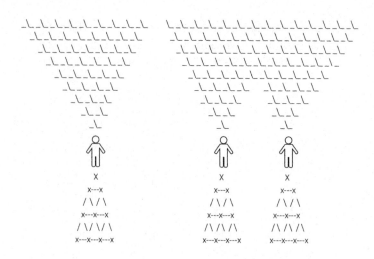

Dialectics is a battle for objective knowledge, wisdom and truth, and therefore for life and death. This is important to remember.

Episteme

Episteme means knowledge and insight of the parts, things, ideas and contexts. Doxa means what people think, as in popular opinion. The epistemic is often in opposition to doxa/belief. Plato in particular is the man behind this division. Believing one has understanding, there is no immediate reason to examen what you think you already know.

The value of someone revealing your wrongness is great. It sets in motion a dialectical process that can be formidable. An idea first always arises in one head only. The thoughts of Heraclitus and Plato have had tremendous cultural-forming significance to this day. Their thoughts were also original at some point.

Techne

Techne often means knowledge such as skill, without necessarily having indepth knowledge of what you are doing. If you possess techne, you are skilled.

Sophrosyne

Sophrosyne means good posture. If you are a leader, citizen, scientist, employee, pupil, student, bureaucrat, you show good attitude. Good attitude is wisdom like honesty, working for what is good and useful, being truthful, and not greedy and selfish. For Plato courage was an important value. Aristotle is known for "the golden mean". Both were common ways of looking at sophrosyne in society.

First principle

First principle is the principle that knowledge is based on knowledge of the constituents, their relations, and everything that pertains to the matter down to the smallest relevant parts.

The next chapter deals with the human conciousness, and how people develop by involvement and factual speech.

4.

Why does it work?

This last chapter is a tribute to man and the free cultures, as people can be free to think and do what they want. People want to participate and be a part of the culture.

Human nature and culture:
_____

What is the driving force behind this logical development plan? Why does this work some places, and not everywhere? First, we must look at the concept/class of man and ask; what is a human being? What is its nature and consciousness, environment and culture, and what significance do these environments have?

By nature, man's brain is in constant search, and by nature curious. That's the way to learn. Our brain and consciousness function dialectically, as it's generally concerned with finding shortcomings, and things it doesn't know.

Human consciousness, thoughts and emotions is concerned with finding meaning, understanding and explanations. Consciousness looks for something it doesn't yet know. It looks for confirmation, things lacking, omissions, and errors. Finding these is the prerequisite for being able to develop and survive.

If our brain hadn't been outward-looking and interested in what is outside of ourselves, we would soon be dead.

It's vital in contact with other people to learn words, and to be reasonable comfortable, to be able to think together.

Sometimes we discover flaws without thinking about it. It's for people that shortcomings and destruction exist. The reality just is, and changes. When consciousness is so naturally questioning, it's because it can't be different. We are not driven by instincts and must have meaning in a shorter or longer perspective.

When we don't learn, what we have in mind corresponds

to what we already know/confirm, or think we know. The problem with humans, is that we are so quick to believe knowing what we don't know. For people "knowing everything", it's a waste of time to be curious, to stop for a second and listen.

In a historical context, open culture facilitated a combination of possibilities, consciousness and nature. Open cultures (democracies) have quickly moved away from other cultures, in terms of knowledge, freedom and improvement, and technology.

The explanation for the success is involvement: goals, communication, knowledge, objectivity, and opportunities. Factual cultures of openness form commitment, knowledge, and growth of ideas.

Under, we see the political power/participation organization of "project Athens". At the top are elected leaders in an absolute relationship of trust with the citizens people/"project participants". Leaders have roles as responsible goal managers; doing what best serves the people and their human nature/freedom.

(The vertical and slash lines, shows that there is communication between them.)

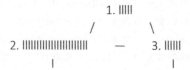

1. Leaders.

2. People's Council; Boule/planning group. Political bureaucracy/Senate for the management of the city, and the people.

3. *Prytanikon;* chairmen/*prytaneia*. Tip office/lunch and resting room (also called *tholos;* round building), open 24/7.

4. The people, are represented in the other bodies, where communication between them is strong.

Between points 3 and 4, there was continuous potential contact 24/7 (open door policy), and once a week the citizens gathered at a juridical equal level (*isonomia)*, as a unity (*Ecclesia*) to present, debate (and vote) at Pnyx; the Athenian Assembly.[1]

The people were ordinary people; artisans, rowers on warships, craftsmen, farmers, soldiers, officers, philosophers, artists, masons, rich people and aristocracy.

Involvement was interdisciplinary, with a rich sharing of thoughts and knowledge in the culture.

The sketch above shows three things at once. It shows the mental understanding of citizens, bureaucracy, leaders, all as of equal status. It shows the organization of power as such in society, where all power, distribution of power, end of power relations, and that decisions of everything that concerns life in the city was debated and decided here. It shows also that project for knowledge and good decisions

---

1 Ecclesia

concerns everyone (citizens), and that they understood that involvement is the means to reach this goal.

Real involvement means that you have the right to speak, that someone listens, that they have an interest, and that you get feedback on your suggestions. Feedback is a normal polite behaviour of confirmation that you are equal, and a recognition that you have spent your time and energy on something you think is important to people.

The break room *(tholos)* (nr. 3) was an open room, where people came in and talked/came with tips/ shortcomings and ideas. The input could not be stopped or "forgotten" by one or a few people.

"What do you want to say, and what can you do?"

Boule

Gr. "Plan"/"meeting":[2] By drawing lots, 500 members, consisting of 1/3 members from coastal demes (villages), city, and inland demes. These were devided into 3, with 1/3 in each *tritty,* meaning 1/3. The trittys, (the 500) were devided into 10 fyles. At 1/10 of the year, each of the 50 were Prytaneis like sort of senators or ministers (in the tholos). So, the Boule consisted of 10 fyles. They sat for one year.

---

2 After Cleisthenes reform.

The city and its citizens were thus seen as consisting of "parts" with interests and experiences. The citizens were assessed differently now compared to pre-democratic time, as important contributors with possible input and participation for the good of the city. Man is an active nature bringing back and contributing, and not only as a mean to power (king/tyrant/aristocrat) as earlier times.

*

A philosophical thinking having great significance for the modern understanding of human nature and consciousness is existentialism.

Existentialism says that man must first exist – to be/form himself. This means that man shapes himself and his person through the way he orients himself and relates to things and people.

Man isn't something that's determined to become/develop in a particular way. The possibilities lie in the genes as potentialities. Whether the environment is so that these possibilities can activate, it's culture and man himself that decides. Or rather, it depends on whether people in positions of power knows what they can contribute to, whether they go beyond their own position, adopt a genuine developmental attitude, and listen to people and those who say they know something.

"To become" means that you form your person, your selfimage, and hopefully your selfconfidence.

It means a lot if you feel welcome, which in turn means that you are allowed and free to talk and contribute.

I see the existentialist's way of looking at man as by nature "open" and questioning in its approach to the world.

Consciousness itself depends on the freedom of possibilities to reach the environment and reality. At best it will find the shortcomings of life, in a natural and questioning process, making an understanding of a whole.

The main point of the existentialist[3] is that human actions are made by the way consciousness works, as engaged in the discovery of defects and lacks, something that is not present, as "nothingness". The "nothingness's" are everywhere in the consciousness, as it "sees" these lacks, as missing (potential) realities. They are the same as the lack and contradictions of Heraclitus, and parousia in Socrates' search for insight. The basis for human actions and thus thinking is engagement, which lies in emotions/pathos, and not in reason/logos.

Man is first and foremost free, as forced to take a stand on other people and reality; to choose relations to this reality. Many are forced to choose unfreedom.

Do you feel stupid, superior, or different? This is what all people have felt.

When you are welcome, less effort is spent on adaptation, with security in a comfortable community. Our own force and positive power can be canalized on other things such as thinking, exercises, improvement, interests, development of talent, search for knowledge, conversations about anything, and thus achieve wellbeing.

People experiences freedom from participation and

---

3 Especially Jean-Paul Sartre.

recognition of being capable. When you experience yourself like the others, you can feel the freedom you are by nature, and "let go." You liberate yourself by using your engagement and interest, regardless of power, fear, and adaptive pressure.

Being able to show oneself as one's person is the very essence of experiencing oneself as one is, in authenticity and harmony with other people.

"Man is doomed to be free"

– JEAN-PAUL SARTRE

(We are forced to continuously take a stand on everything.)

Happiness can be short lived. The desire for harmony and understanding can become an enemy to oneself. It's uncomfortable to stand outside. It's also uncomfortable being the first to say that something is wrong, with fear of ending up "outside." Thus, freedom is both a friend and an enemy.

The need for security in life tricks us. In the need to understand and be part of a community, as almost a community of faith, we often choose not to listen to others who believe something else, forgetting to listen to ourselves.

I think man is so gifted by nature that we can feel when something is wrong. When you opt out of your own critical reaction, you also opt out of yourself. It's a very natural mechanism for "understanding" yourself out of the discomfort. Then you quickly become ideological.

With entrenched beliefs, theories, ideologies and systems, the ability to think critically disappears. Theories, ideologies and thought systems are aides to thinking to the extent that they pretend to give explanations, but deceptive if they function as truths.

Therefore, the harmony of opposites must remain the driving force for the future of all knowledge. Then anything is possible, and you can reach an exponential effect.

An exponential effect occurs where the incremental/ small improvements are in each joint, all the time. The development of computer and communication-technology (from spacetechnology), is an example where it happens quickly, exponentially, multiplied by itself.

Other areas benefit from this general dissemination of knowledge in society; internet and mobile phones, cars, planes, and an almost endless number of products, which in turn increase the level of knowledge within the various areas of knowledge and technology.

We must understand this, and combine disciplines, fields of expertise, product types and industries, creating new ones, with ethics and aesthetics. Then politics, people, companies, societies, and the world will prevail through its challenges.

An extension of the original project of Athenian democracy had four goals. It was to improve ethics through freedom and reason, for material improvement, for strength and safety, and a sustainable future. These are the same goals we have today. To succeed, all ideas for improvement must emerge, in all cultural areas of the free society, at the world agora.

"...and the elegance of our private establishments forms a daily source of pleasure and helps to banish the spleen; while the magnitude of our city draws the produce of the whole world into our harbour, so that to the Athenians the fruits of other countries are as familiar a luxury as those of his own." [4]

– PERICLES

---

4 Pericles, Funeral Oration, Thucydides.

Made in the USA
Coppell, TX
05 March 2024

29773577R00039